Animal Journeys

Migrating with the Monarch Butterfly

Thessaly Catt

PowerKiDS press.

New York

Published in 2011 by The Rosen Publishing Group, Inc.
29 East 21st Street, New York, NY 10010

First Edition

Editor: Amelie von Zumbusch
Book Design: Ashley Burrell

Photo Credits: Cover © www.iStockphoto.com/Jeridu; p. 4 Jim McKinley/Getty Images; pp. 5, 8–9 Werner Van Steen/Getty Images; p. 6 © www.iStockphoto.com/Jim Harrington; pp. 7 (top, bottom), 15, 19 (top), 22 iStockphoto/Thinkstock; p. 10 Travel Ink/Getty Images; p. 11 Shutterstock.com; p. 12 (left) Chico Sanchez/Getty Images; p. 12 (right) © Rene Paik/age fotostock; p. 14 © www.iStockphoto.com/ Parker Deen; p. 16 © www.iStockphoto.com/Bonnie Schupp; p. 17 Jeff Foott/Getty Images; p. 18 Ingo Arndt/Getty Images; p. 19 (bottom) © www.iStockphoto.com/Judy Ledbetter; pp. 20–21 DK Stock/David Deas/Getty Images.

Library of Congress Cataloging-in-Publication Data

Catt, Thessaly.
  Migrating with the monarch butterfly / by Thessaly Catt. — 1st ed.
      p. cm. — (Animal journeys)
  Includes index.
  ISBN 978-1-4488-2546-2 (library binding) — ISBN 978-1-4488-2676-6 (pbk.) — ISBN 978-1-4488-2677-3 (6-pack)
  1. Monarch butterfly—Migration—Juvenile literature. I. Title.
  QL561.D3C37 2011
  595.78'9—dc22
                                2010030647

Manufactured in the United States of America

CPSIA Compliance Information: Batch #WW11PK: For Further Information contact Rosen Publishing, New York, New York at 1-800-237-9932

Contents

Migrating Monarchs

Monarchs are a kind of butterfly. They are migratory. This means that they make long journeys each year. Animals migrate for many reasons, including to find food and to keep safe from **predators**. Monarchs migrate because they cannot live through the winter in cold weather.

Monarchs live mostly in North America. However, the butterflies are also found in South America and Australia. This is because some monarchs got lost while migrating!

These monarch butterflies are in the Mexican state of Michoacán. Huge numbers of monarchs spend the winter in Michoacán.

North American monarchs generally live just four or five weeks. However, each fall, a **generation** of monarchs that lives for seven or eight months is born. These monarchs migrate south for thousands of miles (km) until they reach their winter homes in California or Mexico. In the spring, they return north and **reproduce**. When it is time for monarchs to migrate south again the next fall, their great-great-great grandchildren make the trip.

Orange, Black, and White Wings

Monarch butterflies are insects. This means that they have three body parts. These are a head, a **thorax**, and an **abdomen**. As all butterflies and moths do, monarchs have

Here, you can see this monarch's proboscis. It is the long, curved thing that starts in the middle of the butterfly's head and reaches into the flower.

two pairs of wings growing out of their thoraxes. Monarchs also have one pair of **antennae**. They have three pairs of legs, though they use only the lower two pairs. They suck up **nectar** and water through their **proboscises**.

Monarch butterflies are known for their patterned orange, black, and white wings. A monarch's wings measure about 4 inches (10 cm) across. Adult monarchs generally weigh less than 1 ounce (28 g). They can travel between 50 and 100 miles (80–160 km) in a day.

Male monarch butterflies, such as the top one here, have a spot on each of their back wings. Females, such as the one below the male, do not have these spots.

Winter Ranges

Each fall, monarchs from eastern North America migrate hundreds or thousands of miles (km) to their winter ranges in Mexico's Sierra Madre Mountains. They arrive in Mexico around October and stay until mid-March. The monarchs gather and **hibernate** in forests of fir trees high up in the mountains. These trees, called oyamel fir trees, are 8,000 to 12,000 feet (2,400–3,600 m) above sea level.

The monarchs that live west of the Rocky Mountains migrate down the Pacific coast each fall. They spend the winters hibernating in eucalyptus trees, Monterey pine trees, and Monterey cypress trees near San Diego and Santa Cruz, in California.

During the winter, monarchs gather in such large numbers that they totally cover many of the trees where they are hibernating!

Spring Migration

This butterfly is in Ontario, Canada. Ontario has many flowers for butterflies to feed on in the summer. It gets too cold for them in the winter there, though.

Each March, the monarchs hibernating in Mexico and California start to migrate north. After traveling several hundred miles (km), they reproduce and die. Their children grow up and fly farther north. Each new generation of monarchs born in the spring and summer moves farther north than the last.

By midsummer, monarchs can be found in many parts of the United States and southern Canada. During the summer, monarchs live just four or five weeks. However, the last generation of monarchs born each summer lives longer. These are the butterflies that migrate south each fall. They will not reproduce until after they have hibernated for the winter.

Depending on when and where they become adults, monarch butterflies feed on the nectar of different flowers. This monarch is drinking from a coneflower.

Monarch Butterfly Migration

These monarchs are landing on oyamel fir trees in their Mexican wintering grounds.

The monarchs here are getting ready to spend the winter in Pacific Grove, California.

Right: This map shows the migration of several generations of monarchs. Though most monarchs spend the winter in California or Mexico, scientists have found that a small number spend the winter in Florida, too.

Map Key

Fall Migration

Spring Migration

Wintering Grounds

CANADA

Rocky Mountains

SUMMER

SUMMER

UNITED STATES

SPRING

Atlantic Ocean

Pacific Ocean

MEXICO

Eggs and Larvae

Adult monarchs feed on the nectar of many kinds of flowers. However, they reproduce only near milkweed plants. They lay their tiny eggs on milkweeds because those are the only plants their **larvae** eat.

Monarchs lay many eggs. They most often lay each egg on a different milkweed plant, though. Caterpillars break out of the eggs about four days after they were laid.

This monarch caterpillar is standing on a milkweed flower while it eats a milkweed leaf.

Monarch larvae are also known as caterpillars. After monarch caterpillars hatch, they eat their own eggshells. Then, they eat the milkweed plants on which they hatched. The caterpillars eat a lot. They quickly grow fatter and longer.

Monarch caterpillars have black, yellow, and white stripes on their bodies. They shed their skins several times as they eat. Sometimes, they eat their outgrown skins.

Metamorphosis

A monarch pupa has a gold-colored line and spots on it. Scientists are not sure how or why these gold-colored markings form.

After a monarch caterpillar grows to about 2 inches (5 cm) long, it is ready to go through **metamorphosis**. First, it splits the outside layer of its skin and hangs upside down from a leaf or a branch. Then, it turns itself into a pupa, or chrysalis. The pupa is a waxy green color at first. After about two weeks, it becomes clear.

Then, an adult butterfly comes out of the clear chrysalis. At first, its wings are folded. It uses fluid stored in its abdomen to **inflate** its wings. The butterfly rests while its wings harden and dry. Then, it flies away to feed on the nectar of flowers.

This adult monarch has just broken out of its chrysalis. A monarch most often comes out of its chrysalis in the middle of the morning.

Poison and Predators

Monarch caterpillars and butterflies are poisonous to many animals. This is because the milkweed plants that monarchs feed on as caterpillars have a poison in them.

Milkweed poison does not hurt spiders or bugs as much as it hurts some other animals. For this reason, spiders and bugs do catch and eat some monarchs.

The poison affects most animals' hearts. However, the poison does not hurt the monarchs.

The bright colors of monarch butterflies and caterpillars tell predators to stay away from them. In fact, the predators that generally feed on insects, such as birds and mice, do not often kill monarchs.

This is a milkweed flower. Milkweeds are beautiful plants, but they are poisonous to many animals.

This is a viceroy butterfly. Viceroys look a lot like monarchs. They are poisonous, too. Two animals can develop the same ways to warn off predators. This is known as Müllerian mimicry.

However, there are some birds and mice in Mexico that can eat monarchs without getting sick. These birds and mice kill a large number of hibernating monarchs each year.

Studying Monarchs

No one knows for sure how migrating monarchs know where to go. The monarchs that migrate south each year to their winter homes in California or Mexico have never been there before. Still, these monarchs return to the same trees in the same mountain areas that other monarchs have in past years.

Scientists are very interested in studying how migrating monarchs find their ways to their winter homes and summer ranges. Some scientists think monarchs use Earth's **magnetic field** and the position of the Sun in the sky to figure out where to fly. One way scientists study migrating monarchs is by tagging them with numbered tags. That way, scientists can watch the migratory routes of monarchs.

In schools, kids often raise monarch butterflies to study them as they go through their metamorphoses. Then they let the butterflies go, as this boy is doing.

Saving Monarchs

Scientists worry that many of the monarchs from eastern North America are in danger. Lots of these monarchs are dying. This is because both the forests where monarchs spend the winter and the fields of milkweed where they reproduce in the spring and summer are being cut down.

Scientists at the University of Kansas started a program called Monarch Watch to study monarchs. People across eastern North America help track monarchs for this program.

However, there are groups working to save monarchs' habitats. There are also special preserves, such as Mexico's Monarch Butterfly Biosphere Preserve, where land is set aside for monarchs. Hopefully, this will allow these beautiful butterflies to migrate for years to come.

Glossary

abdomen (AB-duh-mun) The large, back part of an insect's body.

antennae (an-TEH-nee) Thin, rodlike feelers on the heads of certain animals.

generation (jeh-nuh-RAY-shun) All the people or animals that are born around the same time.

hibernate (HY-bur-nayt) To spend the winter in a sleeplike state.

inflate (in-FLAYT) To fill with air and get bigger.

larvae (LAHR-vee) Animals in the early period of life in which they have a wormlike form.

magnetic field (mag-NEH-tik FEELD) A strong force made by currents that flow through metals and other matter.

metamorphosis (meh-tuh-MAWR-fuh-sus) A complete change in form.

nectar (NEK-tur) A sweet liquid found in flowers.

predators (PREH-duh-terz) Animals that kill other animals for food.

proboscises (pruh-BAH-sus-ez) Tubelike mouthparts that insects use to suck in liquid food.

reproduce (ree-pruh-DOOS) To have babies.

thorax (THOR-aks) The middle part of the body of an insect. The wings and legs come from the thorax.

Index

Web Sites

Due to the changing nature of Internet links, PowerKids Press has developed an online list of Web sites related to the subject of this book. This site is updated regularly. Please use this link to access the list:

www.powerkidslinks.com/anjo/butterfl/